MATCHMAKER

Draw a line between each number and its matching symbol.

W9-BDE-603

Answer on page 48

1
2
3
4
5
6
7
8
9
0

#
*
!
)
@
(
%
$
∧
&

Hint on page 46

Illustration: Jim Downer

CIRCUS SHAPES

This circus is full shapes. Each group of shape corresponds to a numb from 1 to 8. For exampl there are 5 triangle

Can you find all the other shapes and fill in the blanks next to the numbers?

Illustration: R. Michael Palan

triangles
1 _____   5 _____
2 _____   6 _____
3 _____   7 _____
4 _____   8 _____

MATHMANIA

5

BACK UP

Hint on page 46

The numbers related to each pair of phrases can be read either forward or backward. For example, "Sweet teenage birthday" is 16, and "The year the United States first put a man into space" is 61. The numbers for this pair are 16, 61. See how many pairs you can identify.

A. Value of a quarter

Cards in a regular deck

B. Baker's dozen

Days in December

C. Sum of the numbers 1 through 6

Items in a dozen

D. 9 + 9

9 × 9

E. Hours in a day

Weeks in a year – 10

F. Roman numeral XIX

Centimeters on a yardstick

G. Letters in the alphabet

The year John Glenn became the first astronaut to orbit Earth

H. Yards on a football field – 6

San Francisco football team's numbers

Answer on page 48

RIDDLE RACK

Answer on page 48

What should you use to add up all the butterflies, wasps, and flying bugs?

Put the words listed below on the rack in order by the number of letters. When all the words are in place, the answer to the riddle will appear in the yellow jars as you read down.

Illustration: Diana Zourelias

additional   calculations   consideration
four   fourth   millions   seventy
subtraction   sum   thousands   three

LOCK 'EM UP

These boats all want to so through the locks of the Ordin Canal. But the harbor mast wants them to go throug in a particular orde

The last boat will go through first.

The first boat will cruise through second.

The boat in the middle will go through third.

The eighth boat will sail through fourth.

The third boat will go through fifth.

The blue boat will go through sixth.

The sixth boat will sail through seventh.

The brown boat will go through eighth.

The seventh boat will be the last to go through.

ut the boats in the right
rder, then write the
tters on their sides in
e blanks to find the
nswer to the riddle.

CONTROL
STATION

Which is the messiest sea creature?

__ __ __ __ __ - __ __ __ __ __

MATHMANIA 9

LEAP FROG

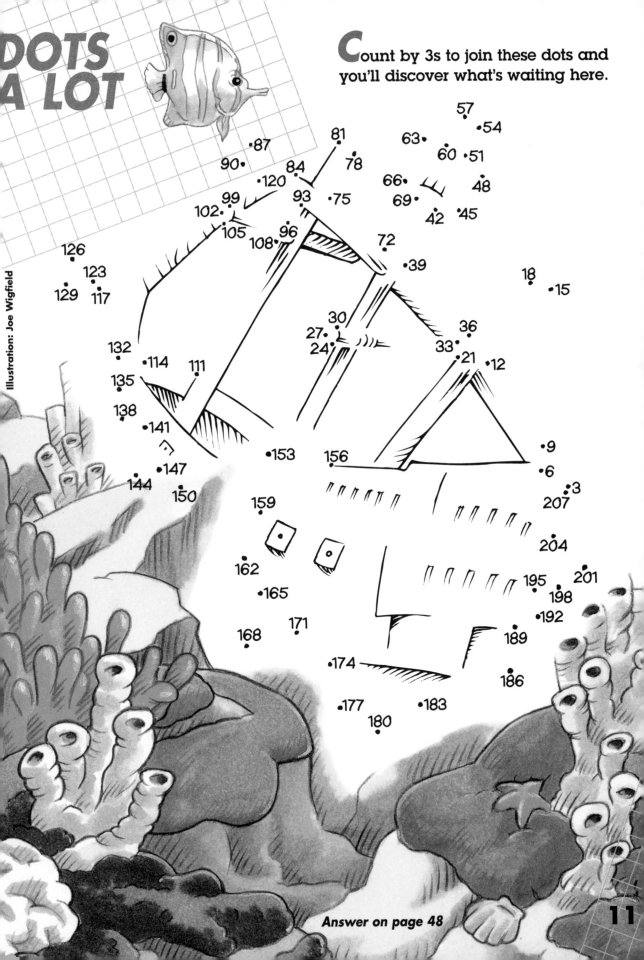

DOTS A LOT

Count by 3s to join these dots and you'll discover what's waiting here.

Illustration: Joe Wigfield

Answer on page 48

11

THE GREAT DIVIDE

Buffalo Bud needs som
help to get back on the trai
He knows if he separate
his shapes properly, he'
get a clue telling him

A

F
H G
O

Divide this square into four quarters using only diagonal lines. Start in the top section and count clockwise. Choose the letters from sections 2 and 3.

B

B C
A Z

Divide this circle in half. Take the letters on the left

Answer on page 49

CATTLE
AUCTION
SATURDAY

LROAD

here he should go. See you've got what it takes to make the marks. Put the letters in order in the blanks below.

Illustration: Rick Geary

C

I T S C K H N O W

Divide this group of triangles into thirds.
Take the letters from the middle third.

D

E O U
R E M

Divide this rectangle into six equal pieces. Starting at the top left corner and moving clockwise, take the letters from sections 2, 4, and 5.

WANTED

"SNAKE EYES"

WANTED

"BAD" DAWG

_ _ _ _ _ _ _ _ _ _ !

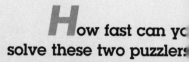

How fast can yo
solve these two puzzlers

A. Change this hexagon into a cube
by drawing only three lines.

B. Divide this watch face into
six parts. Each part must
contain only two numbers,
and all six parts must be
the same value.

Hint
on
page
46

FAMOUS NAME

If you connect the dots in the order listed, you will find the name of the person described in this autobiography.

I was born a long time ago in England. When I was a boy, there were no such things as movies or television. Instead, we saw plays in which men acted out stories of great romance and adventure. I loved the theater and worked hard as an actor and a writer. I wrote many famous plays that have since been made into motion pictures. Some of these include Romeo and Juliet, Hamlet, and The Tempest.

```
     A  B  C  D  E  F  G  H  I  J  K  L  M  N  O  P  Q  R  S  T  U  V
1  .  .  .  .  .  .  .  .  .  .  .  .  .  .  .  .  .  .  .  .  .  .
2  .  .  .  .  .  .  .  .  .  .  .  .  .  .  .  .  .  .  .  .  .  .
3  .  .  .  .  .  .  .  .  .  .  .  .  .  .  .  .  .  .  .  .  .  .
4  .  .  .  .  .  .  .  .  .  .  .  .  .  .  .  .  .  .  .  .  .  .
5  .  .  .  .  .  .  .  .  .  .  .  .  .  .  .  .  .  .  .  .  .  .
   .  .  .  .  .  .  .  .  .  .  .  .  .  .  .  .  .  .  .  .  .  .
```

A4-B4 E4-F4 I4-J4 K4-L4 M4-N4 O4-P4 Q4-R4 S4-T4 U4-V4 A5-B5
C5-D5 E5-F5 I5-J5 K5-L5 M5-N5 O5-P5 Q5-R5 S5-T5 U5-V5 A6-B6
I6-J6 K6-L6 O6-P6 U6-V6 A1-A3 B1-B3 C1-C3 D1-D3 E1-E3 G1-G3
I1-I3 J1-J3 K1-K3 L1-L3 N1-N3 A4-A5 C4-C6 D4-D6 E4-E6 F4-F6
G4-G6 I4-I6 K4-K5 M4-M6 N4-N5 O4-O6 Q4-Q6 R4-R6 S4-S6 T4-T5
U4-U6 L1-M2 M2-N1 B5-B6 G5-H4 G5-H6 L5-L6 S5-T6 J1-K1 J2-K2
A3-C3 E3-F3 G3-H3

Answer on page 49

CASCADES

Answer on page 49

We've given you a[ll]
you need to know
to solve this riddle
Follow the lines tha[t]

16

Connect the boxes, and write the letters in number order in the blanks.

1 2 3 4 5 6 7 8 9 10 11 12

A E E E M N N O R S T T

Where did the lion live?

___ ___ ___ ___ ___ ___
1 2 3 4 5 6

___ ___ ___ ___ ___ ___
7 8 9 10 11 12

COOKIE KIDS

When they got home from school, the Muncher kids were surprised to see a big plate of cookies waiting for them. Can you tell how many cookies were here when they arrived?

Matt Muncher is the eldest, so he took half of all the cookies, plus 1 extra.

Millie Muncher is next eldest, so she took half of what was left, plus 1 extra.

Marsha Muncher was left with 4 cookies.

Hint on page 46

Answer on page 49

PLACE THE PAWNS

Hint on page 46

The king has issued a challenge. He will bestow the title of Puzzle Prince or Princess on whoever is smart enough to solve this puzzle.

Answer on page 49

Place all 8 white pawns on the board so that no 2 pawns are in the same line, column, or row, either across, down, or diagonally. No pawns may be placed in either of the 2 dark diagonal rows. One pawn is in place. The rest is up to you.

DIGIT DOES IT

Someone has been removin the rubber balls from all th local toy stores. That intrep investigator, Inspector Dig is hot on the trail of th bouncing bandit and h

...umbled onto this messy scene.
...he crook tried to cover his
...acks, but he left a note
...ehind. Can you decipher
... and help the Inspector
...ather the clues?

$\overline{1}\ \overline{2}\ \overline{3}\ \overline{4}$ $\overline{5}\ \overline{6}\ \overline{7}\ \overline{8}\ \overline{2}\ \overline{9}\ \overline{10}\ \overline{11}\ \overline{4}$ $\overline{1}\ \overline{5}\ \overline{12}\ \overline{5}\ \overline{10}$,

$\overline{15}\ \overline{2}$ $\overline{16}\ \overline{14}\ \overline{5}\ \overline{9}\ \overline{17}$ $\overline{11}\ \overline{4}$ $\overline{13}\ \overline{11}\ \overline{14}\ \overline{18}\ \overline{18}$

$\overline{6}\ \overline{2}\ \overline{19}\ \overline{2}\ \overline{4}$ $\overline{8}\ \overline{5}\ \overline{9}\ \overline{17}$ $\overline{14}\ \overline{8}$ $\overline{3}\ \overline{18}\ \overline{18}$

$\overline{D}\ \overline{I}$ $\overline{20}\ \overline{3}\ \overline{9}\ \overline{17}\ \overline{7}$ $\overline{5}$ $\overline{1}\ \overline{4}\ \overline{11}\ \overline{8}\ \overline{8}\ \overline{2}\ \overline{1}$.

$\overline{11}\ \overline{21}$ $\overline{22}\ \overline{2}\ \overline{18}\ \overline{18}$, $\overline{10}\ \overline{21}\ \overline{3}\ \overline{10}\ \overline{7}$ $\overline{10}\ \overline{21}\ \overline{2}$

$\overline{22}\ \overline{3}\ \overline{13}$ $\overline{10}\ \overline{21}\ \overline{2}$ $\overline{15}\ \overline{3}\ \overline{18}\ \overline{18}$ $\overline{15}\ \overline{11}\ \overline{14}\ \overline{6}\ \overline{9}\ \overline{2}\ \overline{7}$

$\overline{20}\ \overline{3}\ \overline{9}\ \overline{17}$ $\overline{15}$. $\overline{6}\ \overline{5}\ \overline{23}\ \overline{15}\ \overline{18}\ \overline{2}$

Hint on page 46

Illustration: Joe Boddy

OH, I C'

Answer on page 49

Hint on page 46

Arlene's latest health regime includes a lot of fresh fruit. She trying to keep track of all th vitamin C she gets in a week. F the purpose of this study, she need to eat two whole oranges each da to get the full recommended dail allowance of vitamin C. Can yo help Arlene figure out how man oranges she ate each day On which days did she get 100 of the recommended amount

Monday
Breakfast—1 whole orange
Lunch—$\frac{1}{4}$ of an orange
Snack—$\frac{2}{4}$ of an orange

Tuesday
Breakfast—$\frac{3}{4}$ of an orange
Lunch—$\frac{1}{4}$ of an orange
Snack—1 whole orange

Wednesday
Breakfast—$\frac{3}{4}$ of an orange
Lunch—$\frac{3}{4}$ of an orange
Snack—$\frac{1}{4}$ of an orange

Thursday
Breakfast—1 whole orange
Lunch—$\frac{2}{4}$ of an orange
Snack—$\frac{2}{4}$ of an orange

Friday
Breakfast—$\frac{3}{4}$ of an orange
Lunch—$\frac{1}{4}$ of an orange
Snack—$\frac{2}{4}$ of an orange

DON'T STAIR

The stairway on the side of this old abandoned windmill has 30 steps. On the first step sits 1 pigeon. On the second step sit 2 pigeons. On the third step are 3 pigeons. This continues until the 30th step, where there are 30 pigeons. How fast can you discover how many pigeons there are altogether?

Hint on page 46

Answer on page 49

SCRAMBLED PICTURE

Copy these mixed-up wedges onto the next page to unscramble the picture. The letters an—

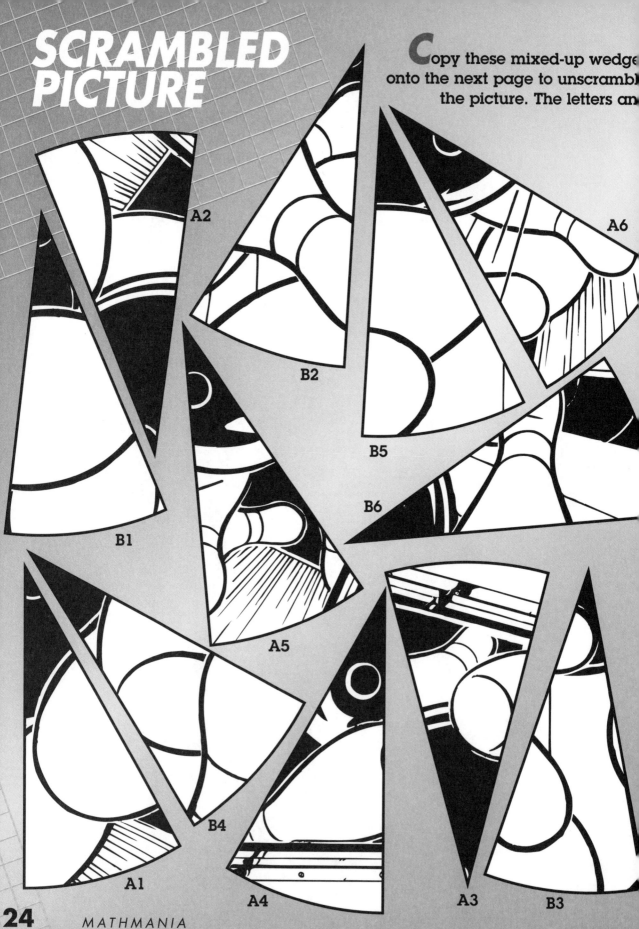

A2

A6

B2

B5

B6

B1

A5

B4

A1

A4

A3

B3

umbers tell you where each
edge belongs. We've done the
rst one, A3, to start you off.

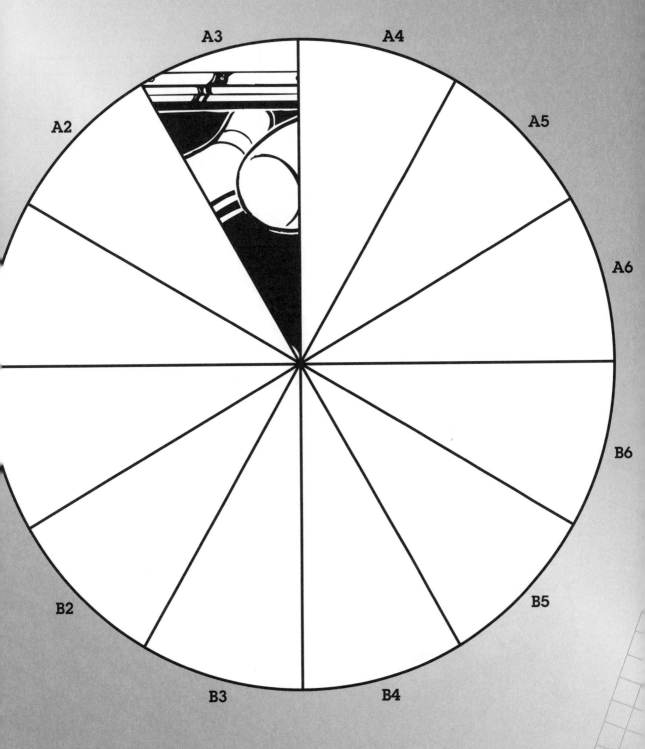

A3   A4

A2   A5

A6

B6

B5

B2

B3   B4

CROSSWORD RIDDLE

Fill in these boxes with the letters of the words that answer each clue or description. When you've completed the grid, rearrange the letters in the yellow and blue boxes to discover the answer to our riddle.

ACROSS

1. Word that means "two people" or "a couple"
6. That girl over there
7. 160 ounces = ___ pounds
8. Good ___ gold
10. Area in which a postal worker delivers the mail
12. Latin prefix meaning "one thousand"
14. Abbreviation for *Social Security*
15. 2000 pounds = 1 ___
17. Make a choice, or a short form of *option*
19. Number of years in seven decades

DOWN

1. Grade between second and fourth
2. All of us together, "___ the people . . ."
3. You can have this ___ that.
4. Postal abbreviation for *Montana*
5. Snake-like fish
8. Abbreviation for *automated teller machines*
9. *Six* in Spanish
11. Number of feet in 20 yards
13. *Two* in Spanish
16. Compass point opposite SW
17. Word that shows position (Put it ___ top of the table.)
18. Abbreviation for *pint*

Answer on page 50

Which two things equal one thing?

SEAT SELECTION

You've got a prime seat for today's ballet. All you've got to do is find the right section, row, and seat numbers that are on your ticket. The section number is a three-digit number, the row number is a two-digit number, and the seat number is a single-digit number.

Illustration: Joe Boddy

Section: _____
Row: _____
Seat: _____

The row number is three times the seat number.

The section number is four times the row number.

Answer on page 50

SIMONE SAYS

Simone wants to remove all the squares from this grid. What is the fewest number of lines she can remove from the inside so that no squares of any size are left? A line is any straight segment between two points, so one long line from side to side is actually four lines.

Hint on page 47

SLIDE GUIDES

Each section of these slide
offers a fun-filled ride. Differen
colored sections allow rider
to go at different speed:

A

C

Hint
on
page
47

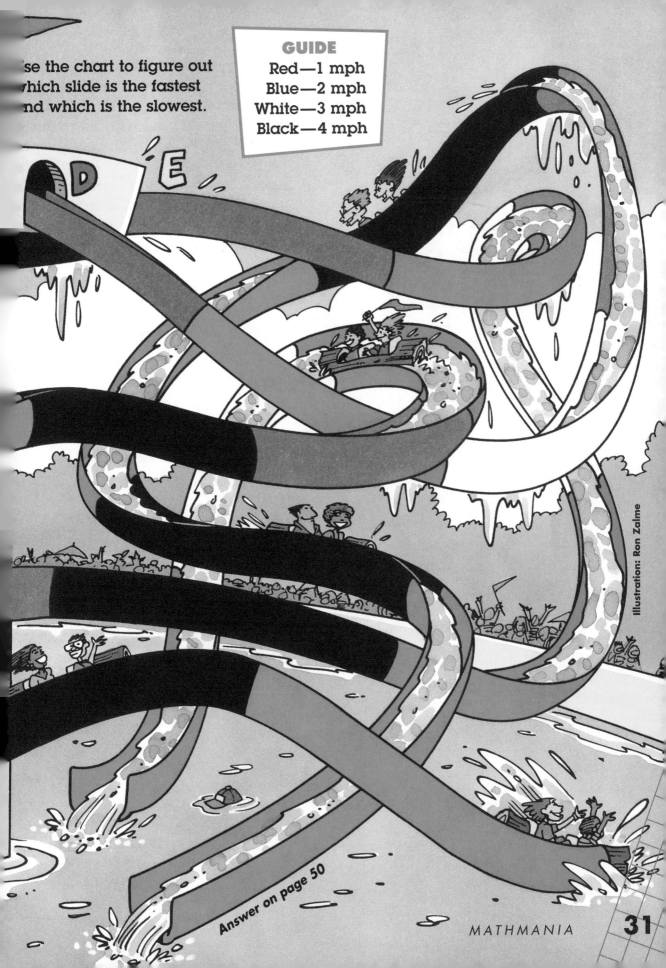

se the chart to figure out
hich slide is the fastest
nd which is the slowest.

Illustration: Ron Zalme

Answer on page 50

LIBRARY LAUGHS

Dewey has some funny books in his library. To check one out, solve each problem. Then go to the shelves to find the volume with the number that matches each answer. Put the matching letter in the blank beside each answer. Read down the letters you've filled in to find the title and author of the book Dewey just finished reading.

Illustration: Scott Peck

Hint on page 47

Answer on page 50

$2 \times 10 =$ _____

$15 + 6 =$ _____

$21 - 3 =$ _____

$28 \div 2 =$ _____

$5 \times 4 =$ _____

$5 + 3 =$ _____

$8 - 3 =$ _____

$22 \div 2 =$ _____

$2 + 3 =$ _____

$29 - 4 =$ _____

$8 - 6 =$ _____

$5 \times 5 =$ _____

$16 - 1 =$ _____

$20 \times 1 =$ _____

$10 + 10 =$ _____

$19 - 4 =$ _____

$8 + 5 =$ _____

$5 \times 3 =$ _____

$8 \div 4 =$ _____

$3 \times 3 =$ _____

$24 \div 2 =$ _____

$4 + 1 =$ _____

SAND ART

Re-create this image without crossing over any lines or removing your pencil from the page.

Answer on page 50

BAR EXAM

Rex and Reyna recyc
a lot of their household tras
The supervisor at the loc
recycling center gave the
these bar graphs to sho

...hem what went on at the ...enter last week. Can you ...elp them read the graphs ...nd figure out the answers ...o their questions?

Answer on page 50

	1 ton	2 tons	3 tons	4 tons	5 tons
MONDAY					
Cans					
Paper					
Plastic					
Glass					
TUESDAY					
Cans					
Paper					
Plastic					
Glass					
WEDNESDAY					
Cans					
Paper					
Plastic					
Glass					
THURSDAY					
Cans					
Paper					
Plastic					
Glass					
FRIDAY					
Cans					
Paper					
Plastic					
Glass					

Which material was recycled the most on Monday? _____

Glass was recycled the most on which day? _____

Cans were recycled the most on which day? _____

Paper was recycled the most on which day? _____

Plastic was recycled the most on which day? _____

True or false: The material that was recycled the most each day was plastic. _____

Were there any days when any material totaled $\frac{1}{2}$-ton weights, such as $1\frac{1}{2}$ or $3\frac{1}{2}$? _____

The smallest amount of recycled material came in on which day? _____

Which two materials were recycled the most last week? _____ _____

Which two materials were recycled the least last week? _____ _____

Hint on page 47

MATHMAGIC

Have a friend secretly write down the day and month of birth. For example, April 4 would be written as 404.

Ask her to multiply the number by 2.

She should add 5 to the new number, then she should multiply this newer number by 50.

Then have her add in her age.

Now ask her to reveal her current number.

The number may look long and confusing, but if you concentrate, you should be able to tell the month and day of her birth, as well as her current age.

Answer on page 51

Illustration: Marc Nade

MATRIX 60

One of the rows, columns, or diagonals of this matrix has five numbers that, when added together, total 60. Which one is it?

1	18	2	16	24
6	14	19	15	7
23	11	0	8	20
21	9	13	17	3
5	10	22	4	12

Answer on page 51

Illustration: John Nez

SELLING OUT

Everything must go fro[m]
the shelves of Marcy[s]
Markdown Market. But co[...]

Countdown Calendar
WAS $98.76
NOW $54.32

Ready Racket Restringer
WAS $33.33
NOW $24.68

Magnetic Tape
WAS $14.67 a roll
NOW $8.89

Used Highlighters
WAS $25.00 a dozen
NOW $20.00

Sock Finder
WAS $56.27
NOW $48.33

Hint on page 47

Marcy's

ou tell which three items
re the ones that were
duced in price the most?

Kitchen Sink
WAS $45.64
NOW $32.99

Purple Polka-dot Paint
WAS $21.14
NOW $16.61

Flapco Flapjack Flipper
WAS $29.99
NOW $21.45

Secondhand Gloves
WAS $31.31
NOW $22.22

Needle Threader
WAS $16.61
NOW $9.17

Illustration: R. Michael Palan

COLD CASH

Hint on page 47

Coach Zamboni is buying new hockey sticks for his team. The price is posted below, but the clerk gave the coach a $3.00 discount for each stick he bought. If the coach gave the clerk $120.00 and got back $3.00 change, how many sticks did he buy?

Answer on page

Illustration: Bill Colrus

Hockey Sticks $12.00 each

COLOR BY SHAPES

Use the key to color the spaces and you'll find a rustic wreck.

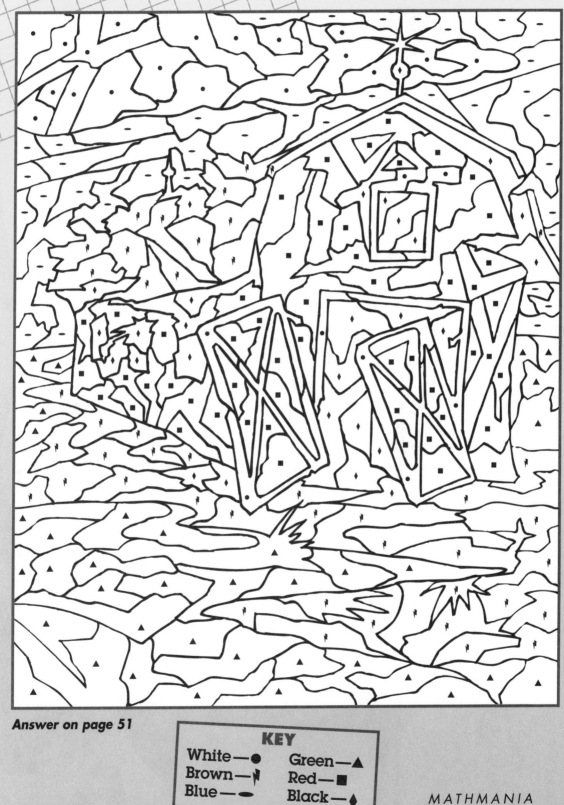

Illustration: Joe Wigfield

Answer on page 51

KEY	
White —●	Green —▲
Brown —↯	Red —■
Blue —➖	Black —◆

NOTHING TO IT

There's nothing t
making these words f
into the grid. Look fo

3 LETTERS

NIL
NIX
NON

4 LETTERS

GONE HOLE LOVE
NADA NONE
NULL VOID
ZERO

5 LETTERS

BLANK
EMPTY
LAPSE
NADIR

6 LETTERS

NAUGHT

7 LETTERS

NOTHING
SHUT OUT

8 LETTERS

GOOSE EGG
OMISSION

Hint
on
page
47

lues in the number of
etters in each word to see
here each word might go.

MATHMANIA

43

PEN PONDER

Justine bought an old barn that was set up for a flock of sheep. It has 8 water buckets and 4 grain bins, as seen here on the blueprint. She now needs 4 pens of equal size and shape for her pigs. Each pen must have 2 water buckets and 1 grain bin. Can you show her how to divide the barn evenly?

Illustration: Rocky Fuller

Answer on page 51

CHEESE WHIZ

You'll be a whiz if you can figure out the weight of the block of cheese on the left.

FULL BLOCK

3/4 BLOCK

3/4 pound

Hint on page 47

Illustration: Jim Downer

Answer on page 51

HINTS AND BRIGHT IDEAS

These hints may help with some of the trickier puzzles.

MATCHMAKER (page 3)
Look at a typewriter or a computer keyboard.

BACK UP (page 6)
Only two-digit numbers are used in this puzzle.

LEAP FROG (page 10)
There are 12 inches in a foot. There are 3 feet in a yard.

QUICK QUIZZES (page 14)
For A, draw all three lines to meet inside the hexagon. For B, the value is 13.

COOKIE KIDS (page 18)
Start with Marsha's number and work backward. She had 4. Millie had two more than Marsha.

PLACE THE PAWNS (page 19)
Each triangular section of 12 blocks will get 2 pawns.

DIGIT DOES IT (pages 20-21)
The word *Inspector* appears in the note's greeting. Use the code numbers from this word to help figure out the rest of the message.

OH, I C (page 22)
To work the fractions, just add the numerators together (the numbers on top). Every time you get 4, that's $\frac{4}{4}$ or 4 quarters, which equals 1 full orange.

DON'T STAIR (page 23)
Try adding the number of pigeons on the 30th step to the number of pigeons on the bottom step. Now add the number of pigeons on the 29th step to the number of pigeons on the 2nd step. Grouping the numbers in this way may make it easier for you.

CROSSWORD RIDDLE (pages 26-27)

You may opt to use words such as *seis*, *dos*, and *ton*. *Milli* is a Latin prefix.

SIMONE SAYS (page 29)

Simone is removing only the lines that are inside the square. That means she will not touch any part of the outer edge.

SLIDE GUIDES (pages 30-31)

It may help you to write the value of each section directly on the slide.

LIBRARY LAUGHS (page 32)

Remember to consult the books to find the letter that matches each number.

BAR EXAM (pages 34-35)

To answer most of the questions, you don't need to worry about exact numbers. Simply compare the lengths of the different bars.

SELLING OUT (pages 38-39)

Subtract all the sale prices from the original prices. Find the three products with the greatest difference.

COLD CASH (page 40)

Figure out the price of each stick by subtracting the discount price from the original price. Now look at how much the coach spent. Divide that number by the cost of a stick.

NOTHING TO IT (pages 42-43)

Only one word is six letters long. Find the boxes for all six letters in the grid.

CHEESE WHIZ (page 45)

On the scale, the $\frac{3}{4}$-pound weight has taken the place of $\frac{1}{4}$ of the cheese. So $\frac{1}{4}$ of the cheese must weigh $\frac{3}{4}$ of 1 pound. How much would the whole block of cheese weigh?

ANSWERS

COVER

MATCHMAKER (page 3)

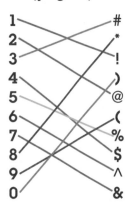

1 — #
2 — *
3 — !
4 —)
5 — @
6 — (
7 — %
8 — $
9 — ^
0 — &

CIRCUS SHAPES (pages 4-5)

1 rectangle 5 triangles
2 crescents 6 cylinders
3 squares 7 stars
4 ovals 8 circles

BACK UP (page 6)

A. 25, 52   B. 13, 31
C. 21, 12   D. 18, 81
E. 24, 42   F. 19, 91
G. 26, 62   H. 94, 49

RIDDLE RACK (page 7)

SUM
FOUR
THREE
FOURTH
SEVENTY
MILLIONS
THOUSANDS
ADDITIONAL
SUBTRACTION
CALCULATIONS
CONSIDERATION

What should you use to add up all the
butterflies, wasps, and flying bugs?
MOTHEMATICS

LOCK 'EM UP (pages 8-9)

Which is the messiest sea creature?
A SLOB-STER

LEAP FROG (page 10)

1 foot 65 inches = 77 inches
5 feet 16 inches = 76 inches
83 inches
4 feet 20 inches = 68 inches
10 feet – 40 inches = 80 inches
7 feet = 84 inches
2 yards 10 inches = 82 inches
The 7-foot ladder is the tallest.

DOTS A LOT (page 11)

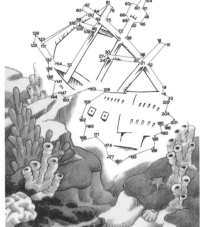